TRAUMATIZED

THE
CONSCIOUS
REALITY

r

by

KRISTIAN·LATIKER

S

Knowledge Is Power Publication

LCCN 2020924802

ISBN 978-1-7363188-0-5 (paperback)

ISBN 978-1-7363188-1-2 (hardback)

ISBN 978-1-7363188-2-9 (e-book)

Dedication

b

I dedicate this book to all who have come before me and all who will come after. Let this be your muse to be free.

Z

Fail to comprehend the streets and you gave up your body now. But fail to comprehend the schools and you gave up your body later.

-Ta-Nehisi Coates

Z

In the end, they stole away everyone and everything that made us strong.

This was The Coming.

-Daniel Black

Contents

Dear Society 1619   *1*

Who Am I   *5*

Angry Black Man   *9*

Adolescent   *11*

Black Boy Fly   *16*

Stereotypes   *20*

Justice   *23*

Division One   *26*

Tunnel Vision   *28*

Routine   *30*

Love   *32*

Soul Love   *35*

To Yours Truly   *38*

Corners   *40*

The Rebuttal   *44*

The Struggle   *46*

How 5 1/2 Girls Tried To Hang Me   *49*

The True Story Of *54*

Doubters   *59*

Congratulations/ Award   *61*

My Conscious Reality   *63*

DEAR SOCIETY 1619

Dear society, I wanted to write you a letter very dear to me and that's been heavy on my heart. This burden and anger on my mind are the injustices and inequalities of the African American people and race. For centuries we have been oppressed, forced onto ships, and brought to an unknown foreign country. Forced into servitude and then slavery, as my ancestors were traded and treated like animals and not even given an ounce of respect.

This issue has been eating at me for the longest. With families broken up, from the cries and screams of babies to the tears and sorrowfulness of mothers. Her little baby is gone, to an unknown place where he or she has to learn new cultures, languages, and customs. Stripped away of their livelihood! Morals, respect, dignity, religion, soul, and all other qualities that define a person. Man! I'm fired up, you almost got me cursing. But in all seriousness, this isn't a joke or a laughing matter. Important as the gray matter is to the brain.

As they tried to strip humans and beings from human beings, the audacity! Thinking they had the right to take this away from us and our ancestors. Giving us a title of 3/5ths. Not even giving us three sips to quench our thirst or our hunger for knowledge. But knowledge came with a price. A price of rope around our necks or a price of scars on our backs. While the ideology of ignorant, inferior, and weak seeps through our wounds with blood staining our skin. As agony screams on our faces, but no sound scurries out.

However, the biggest price was something unintentional and unconscious. The price of generational trauma and hate! So catastrophic, so impossible that it seemed as if devastation was our fate. Submission! Now we are scrambling: Trying to pick up the pieces. Scraping for scraps to make ends meet. Repairing the damages. Playing the surgeon to a high-risk patient. It's heartbreaking when you think about it. Somber, but there is no time to be emotional. Well, not those emotions. We have to have passion and heart! We have to ignite the fire inside of us, expanding the fire to become one. An unstoppable force. We conquer by obtaining knowledge and learning of our true history. Then the pieces will precisely fall in place.

To understand our history. Lift it forward. If not, then what do we really have? What is our Legacy? What is our purpose? We have to use our minds and follow through on the prophecy.

So in conclusion, where are my 40 acres and a mule? And while you all are focused and listening, add the tax to that too, without limitations. I also need my ancestors' reparations without stipulations.

FYI, I do not have any patience,

So P.S., get ready because this Revolution will be televised!

So Recognize!

Kristian Latiker

Z

Why were only our heroes nonviolent?

-Ta-Nehisi Coates

WHO AM I

Who am I?

I get asked this question a lot

But I really don't think there's no need to answer

Because like a cancer

This tumorous disease eats at me

Like cell-to-cell

Like a hell of tales

Burning my flesh and soul

To an endless loop of fear, pain, and trauma

Am I a man?

Am I a child?

Am I considered wild?

A beastly creature

Am I a Black male?

That gets stereotyped for having a darker shade than others

For being wrong all the time but never right

That gets stereotyped for having a stereotype

That gets profiled for not having a profile

Am I a child that has his whole life determined, with two words,

Test scores!

Test scores that get me into college with a lifetime of debt or prison with three hots and cot.

Tests that weren't even set up for us at all

Rigged from the beginning

That western thinking

Am I a Black boy,

That has no father to lead him, guide him, and show him how to be a man?

Am I an adolescent,

That gets stereotyped for either gang banging or caine slagging?

A Thug - The Hate You Give

That is at a constant struggle with oneself on when to be tough, reckless, and wild

Or when to be joyful and have a smile

A savage

An impatient fiend for the white skin

Yearning for a fix

Like Birth of a Nation

When we birthed this nation

A Criminal

That can never be trusted

Ignorant,

Stereotyped for not knowing how to read or write

Illiterate

Mentally retarded

Different

Not like me so I hate you

Not like me so I chase you

Not like me so I rape you

Strange

Like strange fruit

I hang

My neck snaps

PULL!

Hang

Cracks

PULL!

Hang

POPS!

Freeze

Burn!

Maybe I'm Insane,

For being a crack baby

Or from the medicine that Mommy and Daddy said the doctor gave me

Or since my dad put gaping holes in my mom

From hollow tips to hollow trips

Doctor visits to Child Protective Services

Psychoanalysis for my Psychopathic Analysis

Needing an antibiotic for this infection

An antipsychotic for that depression

Inadequate

Insufficient funds

Scares

Impoverished

I don't know, you tell me

As these words speak free

I ask again

Who am I

Shouldn't I decide and be free?

ANGRY BLACK MAN

They say I'm mad at the world

Go figure right

The biggest stereotype there is

An Angry Black Man

But maybe this is true

Maybe I am

Maybe I'm mad at the world

For how I'm treated

Inequalities I deal with every day

Or how I get looked down upon like I'm a crumb on the dirtiest of grounds

Like I'm a peasant: a beastly creature

A killer that was never pushed

Just one more coon they won't have to arrest soon

Because they believe in executions!

Death by firing squad!

So maybe I am angry

Furious

Shouldn't I have the right to express myself?

Express my opinions on this jaded society!

But then again, they say it's not a societal norm

So I rebuttal,

Fuck normality

They say shut up and dribble!

They say you're canceled

They say you can't feel this way

But why can't I feel this way?

How Sway?

I mean isn't this a "FREE COUNTRY"?

Don't I have "First Amendment rights"?

Doesn't the "Constitution apply to me"?

Can I be free?

They say I'm going to end up either dead or in jail

But why can't I be a lawyer?

And maybe go to Yale

As I yell and get on my knees

Crying out in pain and agony

Saying please

Lord help me

Protect me

Lord give me wisdom

So, I can have a strong mind

To get through these hard times

Exhausted and Traumatized

I pause

And close my eyes

ADOLESCENT

They say it takes a village right?

"Yeah, a village for sure"

When all I see is siege

And a city at war

I got a rich soul

But I'm extremely poor

My best friend got shot

I couldn't even mourn

Had to be a man

Had to join the band

Gangland

Rain Man

While these colonizers are playing hangman

With the Fam

Creating a league of their own called the J.J.E

Judge, Jury, and Executioner

Quicksand, I'm in a jam

Sticky shit

Big whips, crack rock, hollow tips

All I see

An introspective perception through these wide brown eyes

Hypnosis

Under a spell

It's a scary movie out here

Like Jeepers Creepers

I got the Bible with the Glock on my side

So, I won't see the reaper

Seeing beakers on the stove

Around four years old

Product

But no environment

Living in this ghetto jungle

Everyday trying to get the first down and not fumble

Loose yards, lose life!

That's just the story of the Black plight

Black life

Not even looking to make it past eighteen

When all the odds are against me

How could another being that looks just like me

really hate me, like they hate me!

Relate me

Brothers right?

Not that simple

When all they see is fucking colors!

Not even the mothers or the fathers

That's what the streets taught us

Play for keeps

Don't speak

Just keep it on you, like you play for the heat

Like a feline, I split the beeline

Tale of two cities

Got to stay ten toes down

Always on my feet

Even though I know the Lord is with me

Mommy and Daddy just got popped

For disputing with cops

Body drops

So mad

So red

That now, I'm shooting at the ops

Body drops

Fuck this and Fuck that

That's all I hear

Suck this and Sip that

That's all I hear

Pop this, Smoke this

Help!

Get your mind clear

So high, mind gone

Can fly to Navy pier
Red and blue lights in my rear
If it's my time, then time's up
No need to fear
Heart dark as coal
Nerves cold as ice
Hate in the eyes
Shots fired
The end is near
No need to cry
Dry your eye
Not even one tear
This is the life of a Black adolescent
I wish I had a different lesson
To see,
I wish I had a different vision
To grow,
I wish I could change the mission
I listen,
I wish I could hear the freedom coming for my life

But this is just the life of a Young, Black, Adolescent
I can stop running...

They say it takes a village, right?

"Yeah, a Village, right"

BLACK BOY FLY

I wish I was a Black boy that flew
Then all of my dreams would come true
Because people really don't understand what I go
through

If I could get away
I would
But I always seem to stick out

Sticking out like a sore thumb
Unwanted

I try to yell for help
However, no one understands my language
Foreign to all

I try to grab a hold, but my hand slips
And goes straight through
Appearing faded like a ghost

I try to climb up
But I repeatedly get pulled back down

Stripping me of my progress

So, I run away
Lungs gasping for air
I try to run as fast as I can

Knowing in my mind
That humanity is on the other side

Life or Death
Freedom or Bondage
Pain or Chains

So, I run
Bursting closer and closer
Sprinting to the finish line

But I trip
They catch me
Cutting my Achilles
As I Heal

I realize
That success is inevitable

As I swallow this unbearable pill
And wipe away invisible tears from my treacle eyes

Knowing that life isn't 100 proof
Life has contradiction

Contradictions of
Impossible
Difficult
Hard
No Way
I Can't
Fear
Failure

I laugh
Uncontrollably
To keep away the thought of crying
Because the pain cuts deep

Intensely
On the other side of the bank
The narrow trees
Through shallow waters

My hand extends
There's Our Journey
Our Path
Our Blueprint
Our Success

Unleashing my spirit
Freeing this caged bird
I Fly!

I Fly high in the sky
Soaring to new lengths
Breaking Cycles
Discovering Life

Writing my own story
Making history

As I glide through the canvas
I illustrate

I am the Black Boy that flew!

STEREOTYPES

What the fuck you looking at

I'm that loudmouth

Cotton-picking

Sambo Nigga you heard about

I'm that slick-talking, big-walking motherfucker

Shit, I am a Motherfucker,

Motherfucker

I'm a watermelon-eating, cornbread-munching, fried-chicken-smacking Nigga

I'm a black coon that will do anything for the white skin, for those white men, that little bitty white plan

That western thinking, that only got us sinking.....

Into generational oppression

Contemplating deep thoughts of depression

Like clockwork

Over and over again

Wait

Over and over again

Is my clock broken?

NO!

Over and over again

In this sin, we call life

Playing the game with a disadvantage

A Catastrophic injury

Not having all the tools to conquer

This constant relapse of cycles

Hating myself so much that hate you

Hating myself so much that I beat you

Hating myself so much that I kill you!

As I say,

Yes sir,

No sir

Yes massa

No massa

But hates his own kind

A spook, who doesn't sit by the door

But on them corners!

Right on that corner on 79th

Or maybe 78th, or 63rd maybe 65th,

Name a street, I'll sip the 5th

As I plead the 5th, for crimes I did not commit

Feeling so bashful and so cloaked with indifference, that I cop a 5th

1st, 2nd, 3rd—5th

As I amend my thoughts

I understand!

Just another body to this cause

Again

I don't think you understand my pain

So again

I'm that spook not by the door but in them fields, crushed in between a jail cell and genocide

With homicide in my conscience

Ready to blast nine shots by two Glocks in a Nigga that looks at me crazy!

From being a crack baby

To selling to crack babies

From whips to chains

To whips to chains

Not knowing why I hate

But deep down inside, I am full of love

Unfortunately, I will never show love

Because I was never shown love

and in the deepest form of honesty, I don't know how to love.

So, with not knowing the stereotypes continue

And forms a mind of its own

Hate!

JUSTICE

I

As I see this police brutality, it has become a reality

As many people are getting hit with these bullets of casualties

And the reality of this reality

And these bullets of casualties

Are

That it's really sad to me

To be

Push to the left

Of this pain of death

Like Trayvon Martin

As I saw a Black boy

With happiness and joy

As he went to the store

Not to get stereotyped

As dangerous and poor

And to be treated like a bore

An animal of sorts

And to be made into a deadly corpus

His body

That lay in the morgue

And his parents

That cried O'Lord

And there tears

That's Filled with the death of there son

And the injustice of justice that goes undone

These tears

They weigh a ton

Like the bullet of the gun

That killed Trayvon Martin and Mike Brown

But the ones that shoot these guns

Are never convicted

But they're the ones who get assisted and enlisted

And the Black boy—

He's the one who gets unlisted and convicted

When he's convicted

He's thrown and twisted

Into just another statistic

So, as I pray

Hoping this police brutality

Will goes away

One Day

As shells of the bullets

Hits me where I laid

II

I say, Ashe,

I mean what else to say

As they kill my brothers and sisters

Feeling like my days are numbered

Just another young Black man

Knowing that things can go left

Easier than they are right

I read and watch

Tragedies, hardship, and inequalities, that never seem to change

So, I flip the page and turn the channel

Sadly!

As I unwilling become desensitized

After every shot,

Every choke, every hit, every knock

Hoping that they won't steal my grandson like they stole Emmett

Damn

So, I close my eyes in defeat

Trying not to picture the demise of the Black body

Dreaming that change will be swiftly

DIVISION ONE

I'm D One

I'm the biggest, baddest person alive

I'm D One

My homies with me and they ready to ride

Because I'm D One

I don't have to worry about studying

What is that?

I'm D One

I'm going to school for free

Fuck that

I'm D One

I don't care if I pass or fail

Haha

I'm D One

I'm going to be All-Conference and All-State because I'm D One

Bell rung

I'm late

So, I'm D One

These females know what's up

Because I'm D One

I'm the leader,

I'm top dog

And you just follow and do what I say!

I'm D One

Shit, what is consent?

I'm D One

It ain't no fun if the homies can't have none

Haha

I'm D One

Man she fine

Man she lying!

I'm D One

No!

You're done!

But what happened?

I thought I was D one

TUNNEL VISION

With the most beautiful cadence you will ever hear:

Down. Set. Hut!

Bursting like a jet going zero to 100

Cutting and shifting,

the Boy had one mission:

Get the first down!

As the Boy clutched the pigskin ball,

The world was in his hands.

However, as he bullied his way to five more yards,

Suddenly a new cadence intervened:

POP TWIST SNAP.

He was down.

The boy's future was no longer set

And his once mansion-sized dreams

Were now reduced to a hut's rubble.

Crushed Leg!

Broken Bones!

Shattered Dreams!

With the most beautiful cadence, you will ever hear: Down. Set. Hut. Bursting like a jet going zero to 100, cutting and shifting, the boy had one mission: To get the first down. As the boy clutched the pigskin ball. The world was in his hands. However, as he bullied his way to five more yards, suddenly a new cadence intervened: POP. TWIST. SNAP. He was down. The young boy's future was no longer set and his once mansion-sized dreams were now reduced to a hut's rubble.

ROUTINE

I workout because I really believe in a strong body, with an even stronger mind

I lift
To keep my spirits up

I push
To keep the demons away

I sprint
To leave death in the dust

I run
To get away from negativity

I Squat
To thicken my plot

I jump
To level up

I leap

To clear barriers and limitations

I pull
To lift up the people around me

I clean
To keep my circle tight and intact

I Plank
To strengthen my core

I breathe in
To obtain knowledge

I breathe out
To release ignorance and fear

But most importantly
I read!
Because my ancestors could not!

Z

That was the only way we knew to love them.
This was The Coming.
-Daniel Black

LOVE

Love can be a beautiful thing

However, love can be the cause of your demise

It can cause lies

But Love can also cause you to rise

Like when you're looking up at the sky

with your big ole eyes

Love can be tempting

Like that thing that you want so bad but you know, it ain't good for you

So you don't get it

And now it's making you empty

Like a knock

On a door that may or may not be opened

So the answer is

That love can be a cancer

Eating at you from head to toe

Unleashing feeling and reaction never felt before

Love is strange like that

So peculiar that you can't explain or define it

However, love is quite easy to discover

But then again, it's not that simple

Love really can be hard to get

Difficult as well as Oxymoronic

A foolish contradiction

Love is weird like that

Once you get it

It's something that you chase for the rest of the race

The strongest addition

The hardest drug to kick

Making you

Always

coming back

for more!

Soul Love

I want you to be my soul sister

And I want to be your soul brother

And frankly, you're gonna be my future child's soul mother

We are going to lay under the cover

And I'm going to tell you

I really don't care about another

As long as we have each other

Because me and you

It's just something divine

As we entwine

Connecting our connection

That third eye

Those brown eyes

Thick thighs

Soft lips

A smooth touch

Wide hips

Curvy and Unique

Natural hair

Thick roots

That flow down to your brain

Your mind

The intellect

It hypnotizes me

To want

To need more and more

Your smile mesmerizes me!

Into having tunnel vision

Only seeing you.

You make the world stop

Taking this galaxy out of rotation

Burning Inferno

You give me life

Making my heart beat fearlessly

With the passion of a million warriors

Love and care

The Understanding

You're my sense of security

In an insecure world

I am your secret admirer

Embracing your body in my arms

Unleashing the fire that burns in you

The desire that you seek out

Sensual from outside-In

However, intimate from the inside-Out

You truly are a sculpture

A Work of Art

Art so magnificent

You're My Masterpiece

You Are My Love Jones

TO YOURS TRULY

Girl, I love you
You're one of a kind
I think about the past ...
When you were mine
Girl, you are so fine
You're kind of a dime
Beautiful
Shit
You are sweeter than wine
That taste
Warm embrace,
I don't want to waste time
Staring in your eyes ...
I think it's a sign
The connection
Affection
I think it's divine
Holy, like matrimony
Maybe it's our anniversary
Like Raphael
On a hook

Of a song

By Tony! Toni Tone

This has to be fate, way more than a date

Possibly, potential soul mates

I don't need it all

I just need you

So I fall on

Bended knee

Let's be together

Eternity

Forever

You and me

Z

It came to teach us we were brothers.

This was The Coming.

-Daniel Black

CORNERS

On them corners, man

Them corners hot, them corners real

Them corners the real deal

Man

But hold on, man, what do these corners fulfill?

Right.....But wait ...

Before you say anything stupid or dumb or just answer at all

Listen man,

I'm about to play this role for a second man

I'm going to be your momma for a second, man

Without all the nagging and the drama, man

I'm about to be your pops for a second, man

Wait dang, my bad dude, you don't even know your pops

Not even for a second, man

I'm about to be your grandma for a second, man

Like the wisdom and knowledge that she tells you and only you because you're respectful and you're the only one there to listen

So when you listen, never forget or disrespect it

I'm going to be that little man in the back of your head while giving you that little nudge of what's right and what's wrong

However not too stern

I'm going to be that minuteman, in a minute, man

So listen, man,

For just a minute man

Why are you on them corners, man?

Is it to get money

Or is it to give money

To that store

That liquor store

With that big ole sign in the front saying

Come on in, man, get some more

Come on in, man, give me some more of that money

Money — of that last week's check

Money in that savings account

Money from baby girl's bank account

That college fund

The Church

That collection plate

Come on, man

Speaking to you

Tempting

Nonnegotiable contracts

A 360 deal

Saying, we can have fun, dude

We don't need nobody

Just me and you, dude

Fun like when you reach the bottom of the bottle

And you have fulfilled all of the swallows

That made you reach the bottom of the bottle

And now you're feeling kind of hollow

But you all good and well, man

You don't need nobody!

Because you're on them corners, man

Dang, what a shame

You on them corners, man

The Rebuttal

Aye hold up, bro
You don't even know me though
To know me though
To see what I see
I've been through some things, dude
You couldn't even be me
But feel free to judge, accuse, look down, and ridicule
Like you don't have skeletons in your closet
Dr. Holier Than Thou
Mr. Perfect
Ms. I Haven't Made a Mistake
But I'm going to let you contemplate
Because I have a lot on my plate
I don't need that at all!
I'm going to be great
So listen to me while I illustrate
These words that I say may be a hot take
But it's the truth and I don't need anyone to translate
To relate
To tell our story
You're actin' like I'm illiterate like I'm not really woke

I'm only on this corner, bro, so I can ease my pain and cope

You're all acting

Like I'm a menace to society

Like I'm the one selling dope

But you won't stop until I end up in a body bag or those big-ass fucking totes

Now I really, really hope

That you listen to what I have to say

But it doesn't matter anyway

I don't need your validation

I'm done talking

Is that ok?

THE STRUGGLE

I never knew a Black boy could just get shot and hit in between the eyes

And a person could not even bat an eye

Not be outraged

Concerned

Not even traumatized

For you not even to realize

What has taken place

What has been done

Another body destroyed

Another soul taken away

Bodies decaying

Returning back into clay

How can you sleep at night?

Tucked in tight

Do you not see the ghost?

Do you not see the demons lurking among you?

Where is the love?

Where is the compassion?

Do you have a heart?

Do you think before you act?

Are you spontaneous?

Do you care about the repercussions of your actions?

How do you have so much evilness and hate inside?

Where does the wickedness come from?

Were you born with this stigma?

Eyes of a maniac

I don't think so

You were taught

It's not you!

Learn

Change!

Grow!

b

Three things you can't escape, death, taxes, and rape!

HOW 5 1/2 GIRLS TRIED TO HANG ME

I use this word "hang" because that's what took place

And people might say I'm canceled,

Again

But I wrote this because my pen creates a safe space

Now this wasn't a literal lynching

And I know, I know, I know

I shouldn't have said that word

Because of all of the pain and hardship it has brought

The baggage of a trillion tears

And it's a trigger word

So, feel triggered because I am

Gazing into the barrel

Even though to me it felt way worse

As these young ladies had full intention of destroying me completely

Disintegrating my existence

When damaged goods were a complete understatement

As women lied on my character

To make a caricature out of me

As I was preparing to be tried and executed in the public eye

Many cheered on

And added unwanted dialogue in the conversation of a conversation that was only meant for two sets of eyes

While they loaded their ammunition

When Twitter was used as a deadly weapon

And Instagram posts hit me like bullets

As I lay there defenseless

Like the shells on the cold concrete

From lies

I wouldn't have wished this on my worse enemy

But enemies they wished

For hurt and hardship

As they prayed on my downfall

Implied hatred

Unknown

As I encountered the evil side of anonymous

As the world taunted me

A fool,

Uttering,

"What does she need to lie for?"

"Why does she need to lie?"

"They aren't lying"

"Fuck you"

"You're a rapist"

"You sexually assaulted my friend"

"I thought you were a leader"

"Weird as hell"

"Sick As Fuck"

Why am I guilty until proven innocent?

Then always guilty

Because no one cares about the truth

My truth

Our truth

When the lie is more entertaining

So, where is my psychiatrist?

Where is my help?

As I felt used

Insecure

Insecure of the security of me

My body

My heart

My soul

Being suffocated with humiliation

Smothered with shame

Drowned with disdain

Strangled with slander

However, I couldn't understand

Why?

But I love Black women

I love women

Why wasn't this reciprocated?

I would die for Black women

I would give everything

Why wasn't this offered to me?

A slew of emotion comes over me at times

Being angered

Saddened

Frustrated

Puzzled

Having to tell my parent details

Of details that did not pertain to them.

But only if I didn't have evidence

Texts

Witnesses

Direct messages

I would probably be another static

And my school

My university

My institution

Well, I'll save that for another day

Because at this moment I can't bear any more pain and disappointment

As I try to nurse my wounds

But there are too many to stitch up

I try to cry

Shed at least one tear

But I physically and mentally can not

Robbing me of my own existence

How could someone have acrimony over

One night

One week

One month

One encounter

When the guidelines were set up from the beginning and consent was the number one priority

I could not understand!

But understanding

Well that shit Is funny as hell

Folly

Strange as fuck

As fuck

Can get you Football Numbers

10, 15, 25 to Life

Now that's the deepest form of plight

As a lie and hatred can really destroy a life

Because if I could go back in time I would

But then again, I wouldn't because everything happens for a reason, right?

And life isn't perfect

But does it make it right to take and destroy a life?

THE TRUE STORY OF ....

As I start to see

What people really are

And what they try to be

I found out that there's no love in the world

and no one ever loved me

So I escape

To a place

Of grace with no race

However, as I see negativity around me

It surrounds me

As a compelling justification of hatefulness with no compassion

This tests me

It tests my faith and my strength

Then I start thinking

Wait .....What is Love

What is self-love

Is it love of oneself

Does it cause good health

Mentally, physically

Is it bad?

Can it make me sad?

A somber tone

Wait

Will I go to jail?

Thinking like this?

Slammed between two cells

My mind wonders......

And wonders....

Stop!

I can't live in this

A type of symbolical, upward psychological hell

So I have to prevail

Then I start to think

Fast

Swift

Swift, like the wind roaring in Chicago on a turbulent afternoon

Thoughts blistering with anguish

Quick

Rapid

Ambient

Instant, like light

Out of sight

And out of mind

But just in time

I'm gonna make it

I'm gonna win

Then I get brought back down again

From our misguided ancestors

Maybe I'm dumb

Maybe I am slow

Maybe I'm like the rest

Maybe I'm not the best

Maybe I'm just a nigga

A coon

A buffoon

A monkey, an ape, a gorilla, a baboon

A beastly savage

With no gauge of lively aspiration

However, I ask myself am I this word that no being should ever utter

With trembling lips of rage

Wicked triggers

Magnified lens

A NIGGER!!!

Feeling like this misunderstood character

Bigger

Mr. Thomas

As I read into these books of books

I ask myself

Am I a Native Son?

And is this really right?

Seeming so close, just not close enough

But still, these cruel and evil derogatory words cut me

Like deep cuts of hatefulness, ignorance, and despair

Every time I hear these words

They take a bit of my

Dignity

Pride

And strength

However, this doubt is just an uncharacteristic mindset

Without a doubt

Then I switch

As I start to think logically

To finish the race and write the prophecy

I'm going to win

I will make it

I am the best

And frankly

I will pass this test

So I redirect my intellect

As I go on this journey to success

I can feel something glorious deep inside my chest

As I go on this challenging quest

I feel a sense of entitlement inside my chest

As I go on this dangerous quest

I feel a sense of power in my chest

As I go on this shaky road

Trying to find that land of gold

Not knowing that gold can be sold

Like a Commodity

Cutting deep as blood stains my pen and sheet of conviction

Like those diamonds sold in Sierra Leone

Trying to educate the masses

Of the true Kings and Queens

That inherited this inhabitant

Seeking to save

The misguided negro

The institutionalized prisoner

The uneducated adolescent

That knowledge is the key to impact, glory, and change

Because we are way more than pawns in this chess game

But as I concluded

this has been a true story of............

A story true that's never been told

DOUBTERS

You can't publish a book

You're not qualified

You can't go on your own

You can't stay by yourself

You're too young

You will never play again

You will never be the same

You can't come back

You're not good

You suck

You're not ready

You will fail

Aren't you scared

Aren't you nervous

That looks hard

It's too hard

You're weird

You're lame

You're different

Why are you asking so many questions?

Stop moving!

Sit your ass down!

Shut up!

Be quiet

Stop talking

You're just a........

OK,

Are you all finished?

Watch me!

CONGRATULATIONS/ AWARD

I want to give a special thanks to all the fathers that never raised us

A shout out to all the females that tried to play us

To all of the real homies that switched up and tried to snake us

As the pitch black, dark black, Egyptian blue sky scurried through the night

The homies went too

Came and went

Like a U-Haul Truck

Day and night

Morning to evening

Breakfast, Lunch, and Dinner

On and off

Like a light switch

On and off

Real homies

Real and True

I want to give a shoutout to all the mothers that didn't want us

Abortion plan B and Adoption plan A

With Poverty Plan C

As the Nightmares really haunt us

I want to give a special thanks to all the mothers that really made us

The church folk who tried to save us

Or how some mothers who tried to "safe" us

From trying to be a man

Not growing up too soon

My little baby

Too soon

To the grandparents who put us on game

The Matriarch

The Patriarch

That family tree

I want to give a round of applause to the teacher that said we weren't going to be shit

To no patience

To disrespect

A huge shoutout to all the coaches that tried to bench us

The professors who tried to fail us

Because failure was all they knew us to be

So thank you

Thank you for that unneeded motivation

MY CONSCIOUS REALITY

I know I live in a world of insanity

As I struggle on, when to gauge the spectrum of my vanity

Realizing that calamity will always come with some type of humanity

They try to

Castrate my dignity

Mutilate my pride

Sterilize me,

While they altered my insides

Unman the hood of my manhood

Dissect my body

Divide

3/5ths

Sex symbol

Only seeing a "Nigger" that's addicted to sex

Assemble

Assemble in three

Mind, Body, and Sou...

No

Genitals

They over sexualize me

Then dehumanize me

As they rape away my innocence

Impregnating me with a bastard ideology

Keeping me in the basement

Keeping us in the dark

Division

Among us

That vision

Amongst us

To live

To survive

To just stay alive

But fuck that!

I'm done just living

I want to strive

I think *this*

I say *this*

I write *this*

For the ones with no hope

For the one

That's the butt of everybody's joke

The little boy

The little girl

The big brother

The big sister

The mother

The father

I do it for you

This is my conscious reality through an unconscious reality

This is for you

Z

But race is the child of racism, not the father.

-Ta-Nehisi Coates

Z

This was not the end. There would be another day.

This was The Coming.

-Daniel Black

ACKNOWLEDGMENTS

I want to take the time and thank everyone who has played a part in my ascension as a black man. I want to thank my church, family, friends, elders, and mentors. Everyone who has ever believed in me or given me a word of wisdom. I want to thank my parents, Karen Newson and Victor Latiker for instilling strong beliefs in me and giving me creative freedom as an adolescent. I want to thank my grandparents, Shirley Newson, Jannet Latiker, and Wille Newson for giving me perspective. Lastly, I want to thank God Almighty. Without God, none of my past, present, and future endeavors would be possible.

Philippians 4:13

ABOUT THE AUTHOR

Kristian Latiker is a canvas to the people using knowledge, words, stories, and truth. Born and raised in Chicago, Illinois, Kristian strives to be the best he can truly be, by creating a safe space using different forms of art and literature. Creating for those who are in need of inspiration and hope.

Business Inquiries and Bookings

>Email: Kristian@getrelocate.com
>Instagram: KrisTheKing__

www.ingramcontent.com/pod-product-compliance
Lightning Source LLC
Chambersburg PA
CBHW021159090426
42740CB00008B/1154